Campagna Books.
Two cousins at the Farm book edition August 2020
Copyright © 2020 by Gisela Foster
All rights reserved. This book or any portion thereof may not be reproduced in whole or in part in any form without the express written permission of the publisher.
For information about special discounts for bulk purchases, please contact Campagna **Books at campagnabooks@outlook.com**
For more information
Printed in the United States of America
First Printing, August 2020
ISBN 978-0-578-23693-3
Campagna Books.

Welcome to our Farm.

I am Charlie and the boy with the hat is my cousin Luis. At our farm, we have one cow

One Cow

Luis enjoys the apple trees where the rabbits play.

At our farm, we have two rabbits

Two Rabbits

Charlie's favorite place on the farm is the field with ponies.

At our farm, we have three ponies

Three Ponies

Luis and Charlie spend a sunny day on the path with the lambs.

At our farm, we have four lambs.

Four Lambs

Luis likes to play near the windmill with the dogs.

At our farm, we have five dogs.

Five Dogs

Charlie spends the morning outside the barn with the cats.

At our farm, we have six cats.

Six Cats

On the farm next to the fence Luis and Charlie find a group of pigs.

At our farm, we have seven pigs.

Seven Pigs

A rainbow appeared while Charlie and Luis play at the barn with the sheep.

At our farm, we have eight sheep.

Eight Sheep

At the coop, Luis likes to feed the chickens.

At our farm, we have nine chickens.

Nine Chickens

At the pond in the front of the house, Luis and Charlie feed the ducks.

At our farm, we have ten ducks.

Ten Ducks

Charlie and Luis love the farm.

You must take time to learn about the animals on the next pages.

At our farm, we practice numbers by counting the animals.

Charlie and **Luis** love the farm.

Cows produce milk.
Rabbits like to jump.
Pony is a small horse.
Lambs are young sheep.
Dog is man's best friend.

Charlie and Luis love the animals.

Cat is a domestic pet.
Pig is a social animal.
Sheep produce wool.
Chickens lay eggs.
Ducks like to swim.

Made in the USA
Columbia, SC
07 August 2020